FAVERSHAM
TO DOVER

Vic Mitchell and Keith Smith

Cover picture: On Mondays to Fridays in the summer of 1951, Canterbury had a Pullman Car service. The 11.30am "Kentish Belle" from Victoria detached coaches at Faversham before continuing to Ramsgate. This is the empty stock arriving at Canterbury East for the return journey, which started at 5.30pm. Ferry vans stand in the down sidings.
(P.Ransome-Wallis)

First Published August 1992

ISBN 1 873793 05 7

© Middleton Press 1992

Typesetting and design
Deborah Goodridge

Published by Middleton Press
Easebourne Lane
Midhurst
West Sussex
GU29 9AZ
Tel: (0730) 813169

Printed & bound by Biddles Ltd,
Guildford and Kings Lynn

CONTENTS

ACKNOWLEDGMENTS

We are very appreciative of the assistance received from many of those mentioned in the credits and also for help given by Mrs J.Baker, R.M.Casserley, Dr. E.Course, A.Dasi-Sutton, G.Croughton, J.Davis, J.B.Horne, J.Horton, Dr. S.Huber, N.Langridge, A.Ll.Lambert, the late F.Newman, J.Petley, D.Pocock, R.Randell, D.Salter, C.Saunders, N.Stanyon, C.Wilson and for our wives' endless assistance.

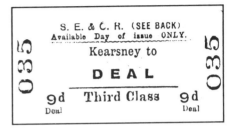

The area map in 1954 shows two recently closed lines with dashes but omits earlier closures. The line to Tilmanstone had not carried passengers for ten years.
(Railway Magazine)

GEOGRAPHICAL SETTING

The route commences on the alluvium and gravels of the Thames Estuary floodplain and climbs steadily onto the gravels of the Thanet Beds, cutting through them in Selling Tunnel. There follows a five mile descent into the valley of the Great Stour to reach Canterbury East, the station here being built on Brickearth.

Several notable cuttings follow in which the line climbs through a variety of deposits to reach Bekesbourne, where it dips to cross the valley of the north-flowing Nail Bourne on a high embankment. Thereafter the route is predominantly on Chalk, climbing to Shepherds Well and then descending through Lydden Tunnel and the short Dour Valley to Dover. As at Brighton, the landform presented constraints and difficulties for the railway constructors.

All maps in this volume are to the scale of 25" to 1 mile, unless otherwise stated.

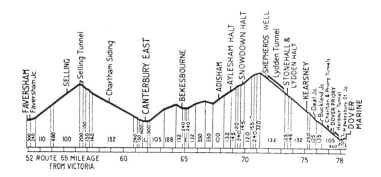

HISTORICAL BACKGROUND

The first lines in the district were those of the South Eastern Railway from Ashford, that to Dover being completed in 1844 and the branch to Ramsgate via Canterbury opening in 1846.

Into this sparse railway network came the East Kent Railway which secured an Act in 1853 for a line from Strood to Canterbury, followed by consent for Canterbury to Dover in 1855. The EKR became the London, Chatham and Dover Railway in 1859, having opened the Chatham - Faversham section on 25th January 1858. Its openings proceeded as follows -

Faversham Creek Branch	12th April 1860
Faversham - Canterbury	9th July 1860
Faversham - Whitstable	1st August 1860
Canterbury - Dover Town	22nd July 1861
Dover Town - Harbour	1st November 1861
Calais shipping service	1st July 1862

The LCDR and SER opened a joint line between Dover and Deal on 15th June 1881 and a connection to Kearsney came into use on 1st July 1882 (closed on 7th December 1980). From 1st January 1899, the two companies were under the control of a managing committee, becoming known as the South Eastern and Chatham Railway.

Colleries were established in south-east Kent just prior to World War I, the route being well placed to serve several of them. The East Kent Light Railway was formed to connect some others to the main line, traffic commencing in 1911. Passenger trains ran from 1916 to 1948.

The Southern Railway took control of the route in 1923, it in turn becoming part of the Southern Region of British Railways in 1948.

PASSENGER SERVICES

The August 1860 timetable showed eight weekday and four Sunday trains. By November 1862, there were eleven and six respectively, of which five and four were stopping trains.

In 1892, the weekday service comprised six expresses and six stoppers. There were also five trains from Kearsney to Deal. After the formation of the SECR in 1899, services declined, as much of the Dover traffic was transferred to the Folkestone route. By 1910 there were four fast and eleven stopping trains on weekdays, with two and three respectively on Sundays. By 1923 there were only two fast trains on weekdays and many of the local trains started out at Faversham, where they made connections with London - Ramsgate services. Since 1899 the Thanet route had been regarded as the main line and that to Dover as a branch.

The Kearsney - Deal service steadily declined and ceased in the mid-1930s.

As the Kent coalfield developed in the 1920s, so did the local passenger traffic. Consequently additional stopping trains were worked between Canterbury and Dover. In 1938 there were 18 weekday and 7 Sunday trains, most of them calling at all stations. Despite the restrictions of WWII, the 1941 timetable showed 21 weekday and 8 Sunday journeys, calling at all stations. A similar frequency was maintained until the advent of electrification in 1959.

The first electric timetable showed a Sheerness - Dover Priory all-stations train each hour together with a fast from Victoria, calling at Canterbury East, Adisham, Aylesham Halt, Shepherds Well and Kearsney. In 1968 the service was reduced to one stopping train hourly, this being extended to Dover Marine in 1970.

In May 1973 a Victoria - Canterbury East hourly fast train was added and this was extended to Dover Marine from May 1974. The stopping train terminated at Dover Priory, except from 1986 to 1988.

A weekday Liverpool - Dover train (calling at Faversham and Canterbury East) commenced in May 1988 and was still running in 1992.

Handbill No. 86.   SE&CR

Commencing on June 17th, and until further notice.

Cheap Return Tickets
WILL BE ISSUED
EVERY SATURDAY
To Shopping Centres

AS UNDER

FROM	TO	Return Fares, 3rd Cl.		By Trains at
Adisham		1	2	3.14 p.m.
Bekesbourne ...		0	8	3.20 p.m.
Selling		1	3	1.24 p.m.
Shepherd's Well	CANTER- BURY EAST	2	0	3.2 p.m.
Snowdown Halt		1	7	3.8 p.m.
Stonehall Halt ...		2	3	2.56 p.m.
Teynham		2	9	1.5 p.m.

London Bridge Station,   P. C. Tempest, General Manager.
May 31st, 1922.

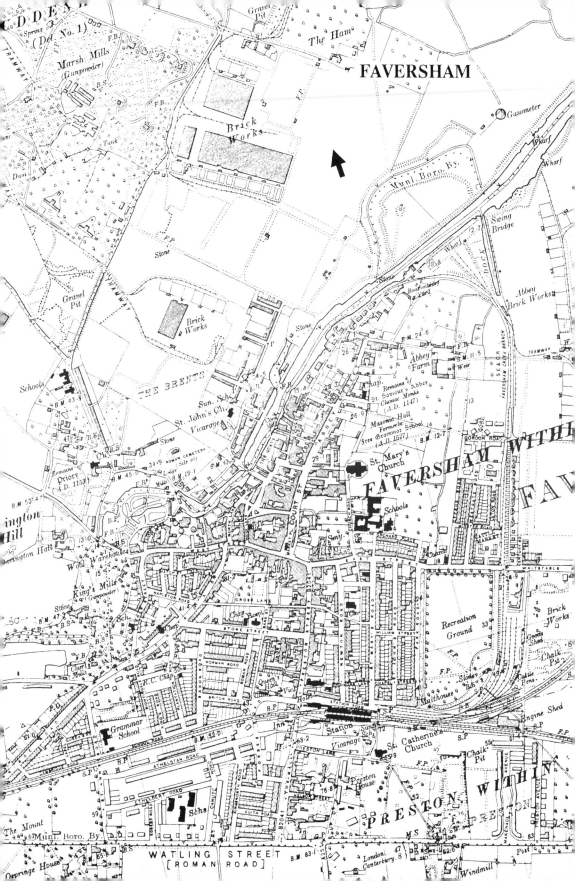

1. A poor quality, but important, photograph shows the first station which was demolished in late 1897. There was another bay platform on the up side and this also faced east. The goods shed was also demolished at this time - its unusual position (at a right angle to the main line) is seen on the 1881 map. The 1891 built 4-4-0 class M3 no. 188 heads the down "Granville Express", which was named after the large hotel adjacent to Ramsgate Harbour station. (Fleur de Lis Heritage Centre)

The 1909 map at 6" to 1 mile has some revisions to 1938. It includes the full length of the Faversham Creek Branch and some of the industrial tramways north of the town, these running off the map to a wharf on Oare Creek. The line from London is on the left and that to Dover is right (lower), with the Ramsgate branch above it. The 1882 edition can be seen in our *Sittingbourne to Ramsgate* album, along with other photographs of the station.

2. The new station had entrances and booking offices on both sides. This is Station Road and the north entrance, which is still in use, although direct access to the south side has been possible again since 1990, when ticket inspection became random. The arrangement of the down starting signals remained unchanged until their removal. (Lens of Sutton)

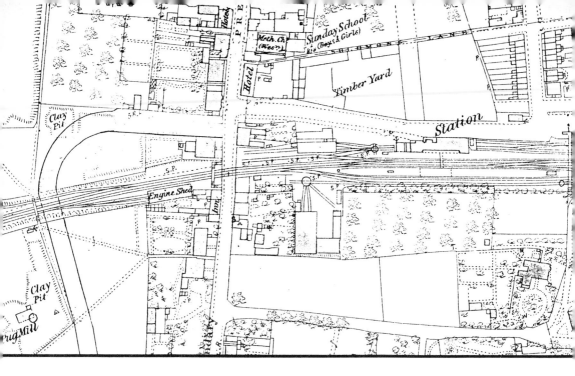

3. After the 1897-98 rebuilding four through platforms were available, greatly easing the chore of changing trains. Dover trains generally used the south side of each island platform. No. 188 is seen again after completion of the rebuilding. (Lens of Sutton)

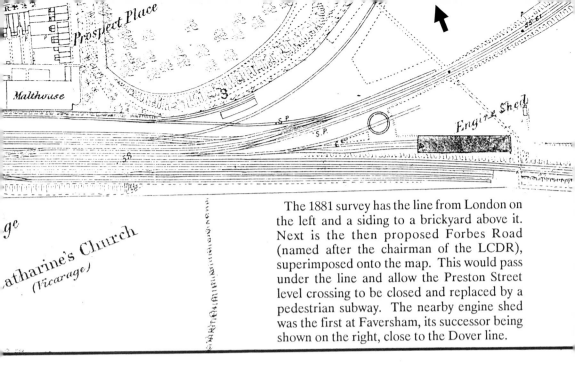

Prospect Place

Malthouse

S.P.

S.P.

Engine Shed

...ge

...atharine's Church
(Vicarage)

The 1881 survey has the line from London on the left and a siding to a brickyard above it. Next is the then proposed Forbes Road (named after the chairman of the LCDR), superimposed onto the map. This would pass under the line and allow the Preston Street level crossing to be closed and replaced by a pedestrian subway. The nearby engine shed was the first at Faversham, its successor being shown on the right, close to the Dover line.

4. "B" box is on the right, and the locomotive shed is in the distance, as steam prepares to bow out in 1959. Shepherd Neame's maltings (now converted to residential use) are on the left. The brewers, who had their own siding for many years, sponsored the renovation of the station in 1989. On the left is class L 4-4-0 no. 31764. (Prof.H.P.White)

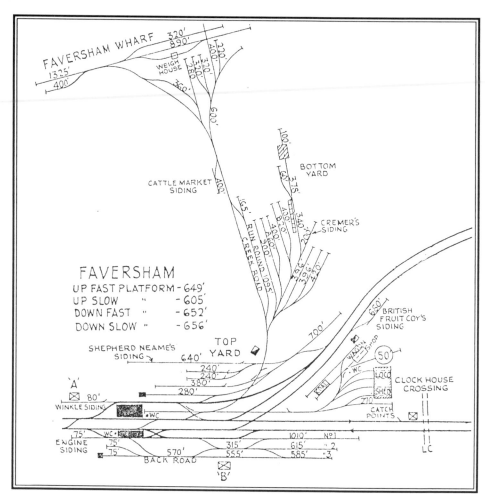

FAVERSHAM WHARF

BOTTOM YARD

CATTLE MARKET SIDING

CREMER'S SIDING

RUN ROUND ROAD

CREEK ROAD

FAVERSHAM
UP FAST PLATFORM - 649'
UP SLOW   "   - 605'
DOWN FAST "   - 652'
DOWN SLOW "   - 656'

BRITISH FRUIT COY'S SIDING

SHEPHERD NEAME'S SIDING

TOP YARD

CLOCK HOUSE CROSSING

LOCO SHED

CATCH POINTS

'A'

WINKLE SIDING

WC

ENGINE SIDING

BACK ROAD

'B'

No 1
No 2
No 3

LC

The control diagram dates from WWII and shows the main line signal boxes as "A" and "B". WC indicates a water column. Clock House crossing is more than a mile from Faversham and was fitted with automatic half barriers on 14th May 1966.

6. The double arms in the "off" position indicated that shunting could proceed between the two parts of Top Yard. Class C no. 31256 stands close to Yard Box on 30th September 1958. Faversham Creek Branch is to the left of the engine in the background. General goods traffic ceased on 16th August 1971.
(R.C.Riley)

5. The new signal box is nearing completion as class L no. 31766 arrives with the 1.05pm Dover Priory to Faversham on 3rd September 1958. The box came into use on 24th May 1959, when colour light signalling was introduced. (P.Hay)

7. Prior to electrification many new drivers (or motormen as they were earlier designated) had to be trained. Class H no. 31522 departs on 21st March 1959 with a route learning special to Dover. Similar train formations ran to Herne Bay in 1953, following line closure due to flood damage in the Reculvers area. (S.C.Nash)

8. Dover bound on 18th May 1959 is N1 class 2-6-0 no. 31879, its exhaust obscuring the junction. On the right is the locomotive depot, while two of the three carriage sidings can be seen on the left. The shed has received listed building status. (A.E.Bennett)

9. The 09.53 Victoria to Ramsgate is seen on 7th September 1988, when unit no. 1596 still retained its "jaffa cake" livery. By then the water tower was a "des res", complete with a roof-top garden - hence the railings. (J.Scrace)

10. As was common at many depots, atmospheric pollution made photography less than satisfactory. On shed on 13th March 1926 were nos. 99, 463, 13 and 379, by then all bearing the prefix A. The building on the left was used for wagon repairs. (H.C.Casserley)

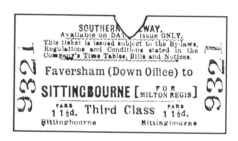

11.

SOUTHERN RAILWAY.
Available on DAY of Issue ONLY.
This ticket is issued subject to the By-laws,
Regulations and Conditions stated in the
Company's Time Tables, Bills and Notices.
9321
Faversham (Down Office) to
SITTINGBOURNE [MILTON REGIS]
FARE 1 1½d. Third Class FARE 1 1½d.
Sittingbourne   Sittingbourne
932

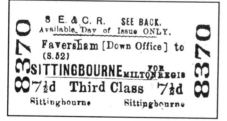

S E.& C. R.   SEE BACK.
Available Day of Issue ONLY.
8370
Faversham [Down Office] to
(S.52)
SITTINGBOURNE MILTON FOR REGIS
7½d   Third Class   7½d
Sittingbourne.   Sittingbourne.
8370

12. The offices and the northern shed were retained for use as a diesel depot until March 1968. The shed was the younger of the two and had been reroofed with corrugated asbestos in about 1948. (C.Hall)

11. Class C no. 1063 is on the up Dover line on 30th June 1934, while its reflection appears in the coach panelling. The right shed was the older and dates from 1860, when the line to Canterbury opened. (H.C.Casserley)

FAVERSHAM CREEK BRANCH

13. An SECR 4-4-0 is on the wharf as coastal ships are moored alongside. Some LCDR locomotives arrived here by sea - two from R.W.Hawthorn of Newcastle-upon-Tyne in 1860 and six from Holland in 1861. Regular traffic included coal, fertilisers, grain, bricks and explosives. In the 1890s there were an average of 25 vessels coming and going daily, carrying nearly half a million tons of merchandise annually.
(Fleur de Lis Heritage Centre)

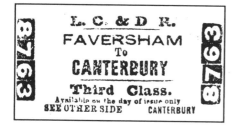

14. Wagons descended into the creek on occasions, having escaped from a shunter at Faversham and gained momentum on the falling gradient of the one mile long branch. In December 1920, class 01 no. 46 presented a greater recovery problem at Iron Wharf. (Fleur de Lis Heritage Centre)

15. Considerable quantities of timber were imported from Norway. This consignment is probably pit props as pulp wood usually went direct to the paper mills. Alternatively, it may be cordwood for use in the local gunpowder factories as charcoal. This is an April 1933 upstream view of Iron Wharf. (L.Catchpole)

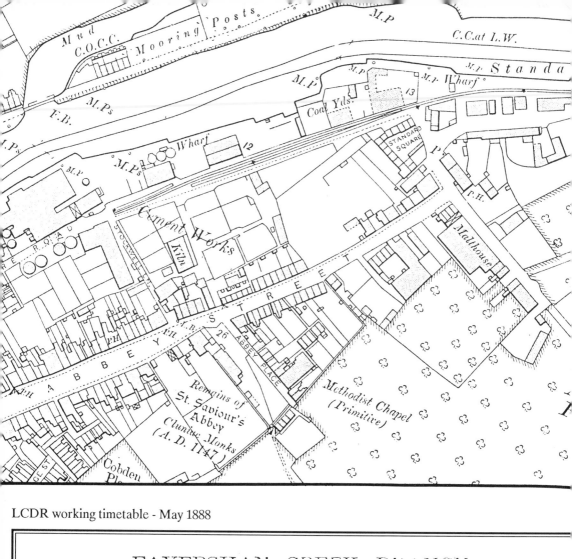

LCDR working timetable - May 1888

FAVERSHAM CREEK BRANCH.

Goods Trains will run, if required, on Week-days as under:—

	a.m.	p.m.
Faversham, dep. for Creek	10 0	3 30
Faversham, arr. from Creek	10 45	4 15

FAVERSHAM CATTLE MARKET.

On Cattle Market days (every first and third Tuesday in the month) the Faversham Creek Line will be used from 7.0 a.m. until 4.0 p.m. solely by the Goods Department, and the Ballast Train must not allowed to work on the Line between those hours.

FAVERSHAM CREEK BRANCH.

Goods Trains will run, if required, on Week-days as under:—

	a.m.	p.m.
Faversham, dep. for Creek	10 0	3 30
Faversham, arr. from Creek	10 45	4 15

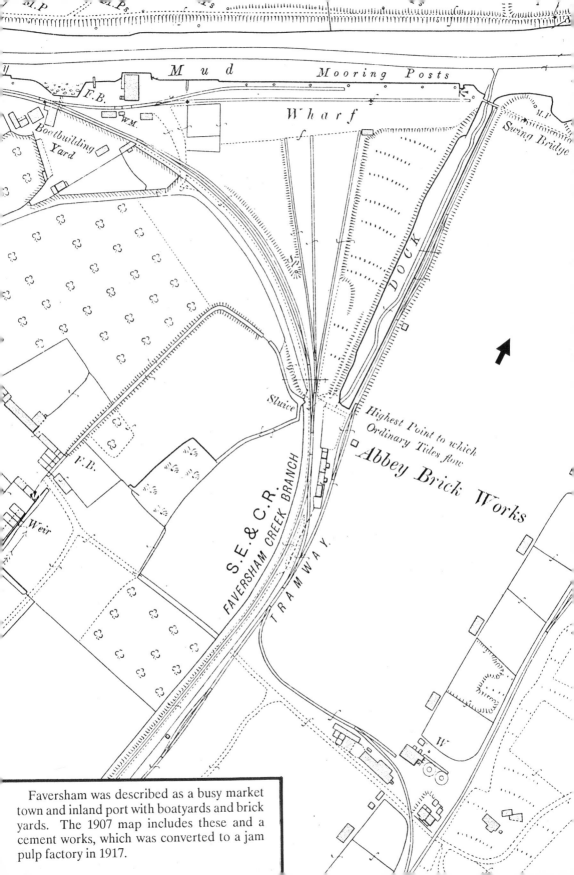

Faversham was described as a busy market town and inland port with boatyards and brick yards. The 1907 map includes these and a cement works, which was converted to a jam pulp factory in 1917.

16. The creek and Iron Wharf are in the background in this northward view, the line to Standard Quay curving to the left. This 1962 picture includes disused rolling stock. (A.Percival)

17. An August 1962 record of Standard Quay shows the downstream view of the United Fertilisers store from the site of the former coal yard. All buildings are now listed structures and extant although the track on the quay was lifted in 1967. (A.Percival)

SELLING

18. Opened with the line, the main function of the station was to serve the agricultural community, hence the extensive sidings and large goods shed, visible beyond the signal box. The station was renamed "Chillingbourne" briefly in 1944, during the making of a film entitled "Canterbury Tale". This postcard was used on 9th April 1902. (K.Elks coll.)

The 1874 survey shows a layout which changed little over the years. The down siding was lengthened and the two on the up siding were connected at the south end for some time.

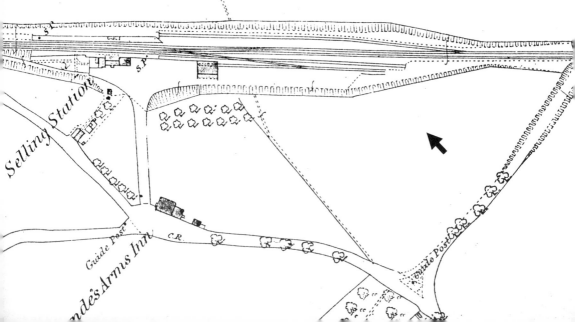

THE STATION, SELLING.

19. The main buildings were on the up side and the station master's house was adjacent. Extreme left are bundles of hop pockets, massive sacks into which hops are compressed for transport. The architecture did not compare favourably with that further down the line. (Lens of Sutton)

20. The footbridge was erected in about 1907 to carry a public footpath as well as being for the benefit of passengers. The path previously crossed the main lines and the goods yard on the level. The goods dock is on the left. (Lens of Sutton)

21. Hordes of Londoners *"of the lower order"* arrived each summer for hop picking, an entire train being hired by a farmer in the early years. Reduced rate travel was agreed by the Hop Marketing Board and the railway ran special trains. The oldest stock was always used, as the rough characters often left it in an insanitary condition. (M.Berry coll.)

22. Many arrived drunk or hungry and would be given tea in the station yard by the farmer's staff. The farmer also provided accommodation (huts in the fields), bedding (straw on the floor), refreshments (water in 120 gallon barrels) and transport (cart, as seen). The pickers brought their own food hampers, chairs and contagious diseases. (M.Berry coll.)

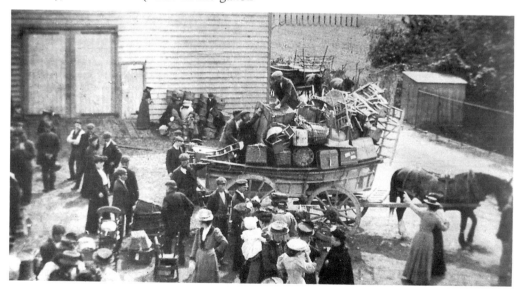

23. With platforms extended and conductor rails in place, Selling is seen in its last full year of steam. Class N1 no. 31822 waits with the 11.50am Victoria to Dover, no. 173 indicating the duty number. This was one of Hither Green's few passenger turns, the reporting number (6) being displayed on Summer Saturdays and other busy days. A further climb of about a mile would take the train through Selling Tunnel (405 yds), which is at the beginning of the five mile descent to Canterbury. (J.H.Aston)

24. Photographed in 1975, the up and down buildings were little changed in 1992 and the down refuge siding was still in situ. The population of the district has fluctuated considerably. It rose following the arrival of the railway and then fell to about 800 in 1881. In 1981 it was 443. By 1992 the station was only staffed on weekday mornings. (J.Scrace)

Chartham public siding was a half mile north of the village which had a SER station at its centre, so no passenger provisions were made here. The siding closed on 2nd March 1961 and the level crossing was renamed Chartham Hatch on 14th May 1966, when it was fitted with automatic half barriers. (L.K. stands for lime kiln).

CANTERBURY "A" JUNCTION

25. The 9.35am Victoria to Ramsgate via Margate diverges from the ex-LCDR route from Faversham to take the temporary spur to the former SER line to Canterbury West. This connection was first opened on 5th May 1918 to facilitate movements of military traffic to and from Richborough Port. It was a single line when closed on 21st November 1924, the track remaining in place until 1935. It was reinstated for military use only between 2nd March 1941 and 21st October 1951. Following serious flood damage to the line between Herne Bay and Whitstable, a double track connection was opened on 22nd February 1953 to convey diverted Thanet services. (D.Cullum)

26. Canterbury Cathedral is in the background as class D1 no. 31492 heads north on 9th May 1953, with the 5.15 pm Dover Priory to Gillingham. The temporary connection (left) ceased to be used regularly on 21st May of that year, when the flood damage repairs were completed. The spur remained usable until 4th March 1956. (J.J.Smith)

27. Passing over the 1846 SER route on 19th April 1953 is no. 35026 *Lamport & Holt Line*, with the 2.30pm Dover Marine to Victoria. On the right is the then disused Harbledown Junction signal box at the northern end of the closed Elham Valley line from Folkestone. The rear of the train is passing over the Great Stour. (S.C.Nash)

CANTERBURY EAST

28. The LCDR sign which frames the station roof includes the words "Ludgate, Holborn Viaduct and Victoria", these being the company's principal London stations. The suffix "East" was added in 1899. (D.Collyer coll.)

The 1907 map shows that the site was not capable of further expansion. After 1899 Canterbury West was developed as the principal freight depot. Look for the numerous wagon turntables and the locomotive shed.

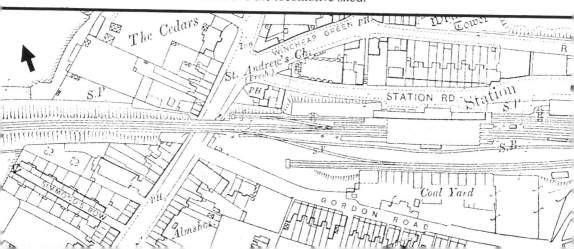

29. A southward view in the summer of 1921 emphasises the gloom that was created by an overall roof. Other features of the period are gas lights and milk churns. (H.J.Patterson-Rutherford)

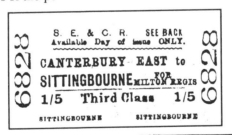

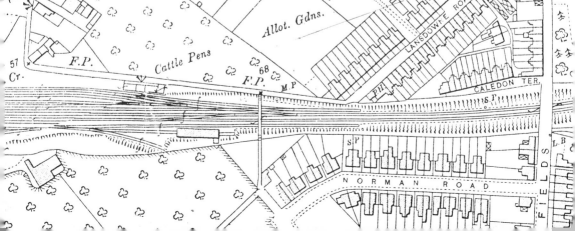

30. A 1924 northward view reveals that six-wheeled coaches were still common, many probably dating from the LCDR era. Also evident are the white painted cattle pens and the goods yard crane which was rated at 7 tons capacity. (D.Cullum coll.)

31. Beyond the far end of the down platform is the white buffer stop of "down siding west", which was removed late in 1958. The other sidings were in use until 13th September 1965, when general goods traffic was concentrated on the West Station. (D.Cullum)

32. Class 4 2-6-4T no. 42075 arrives with the 3.19pm from Dover on 19th July 1958, the roof having lost its sheeting prior to demolition. Milk churns were a rarity at main line stations by this date. (J.H.Aston)

33. By 6th September 1958 the roof trusses had been removed and platform lengthening was complete. Class L1 4-4-0 no. 31754 waits to depart for London, the signal arm beckoning from two former running rails. (P.Hay)

34. The "new" platform canopies are seen on 23rd May 1959, these having been brought from Lullingstone near Eynsford, where a new station was built but never opened. In the distance is the then new loop which allowed a 4-car electric train to be set aside while a fast boat train overtook it. (A.E.Bennett)

35. The 12.36pm Sheerness to Dover Priory was worked by 4CEP no. 7146 on 2nd July 1959, the entire electric fleet being painted green initially. The austere platform canopies were fitted with gas lights and did not compliment the fine architecture of the cathedral city. (J.H.Aston)

36. The diverted "Golden Arrow" approaches the 1 in 105 climb from the station on 26th February 1961, hauled by D6538 and D5003. The second signal arm was added when the electrified loop came into use in 1959. On the right, the former goods shed had been extended to form Cadbury's Chocolate distribution depot. (S.C.Nash)

37. A 1990 view shows that the unimposing exterior has been refurbished and the LCDR signal box (left) was still in use. In 1992 some of its 28 levers were still operating several semaphore signals. (J.Scrace)

BEKESBOURNE

38. For the first 60 years of the line, the population of the village was under 400, although the 1861 figures were inflated by about 100, due to the presence of construction workers. In 1981 the figure was 445. Platform extension was in hand as class L1 arrived with the 12.6 pm Faversham to Dover on 2nd August 1958. (J.H.Aston)

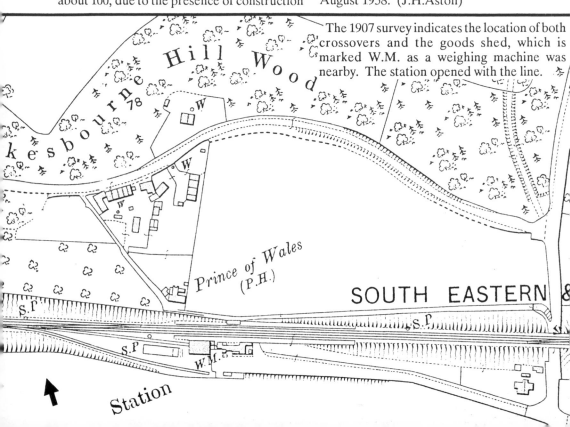

The 1907 survey indicates the location of both crossovers and the goods shed, which is marked W.M. as a weighing machine was nearby. The station opened with the line.

39. On the same day class N1 2-6-0 no. 31822 blows off as she descends from the summit west of the station and brakes the 12.3pm from Chatham. A van stands in one of the two sidings used mainly for loading fruit and un- loading coal, fruit boxes and chips for packing fruit. The boards on the platform form the roof to the rodding tunnel to the signal box. (J.H.Aston)

40. Goods traffic ceased on 5th June 1961, the signal box closed on 18th October 1964, staffing ceased on 14th April 1969 and all buildings were subsequently demolished. This picture of the 12.23 Victoria to Dover Priory on 6th September 1988 includes one of the two footpaths to the down platform. Doubtless additional traffic resulted from the horse racing on Barham Downs in the 19th century and from nearby airfields in both world wars. (J.Scrace)

ADISHAM

41. The SECR poster boards were advertising day trips to Margate or Boulogne while machines offered chocolate or a weight indication. In the less peaceful days of WWII, a 9.2" rail mounted gun stood in a siding at the north end of this platform. (Lens of Sutton)

The 1907 edition should be read in conjunction with picture 42, as it is not clear that the up loop does not come off the up main line.

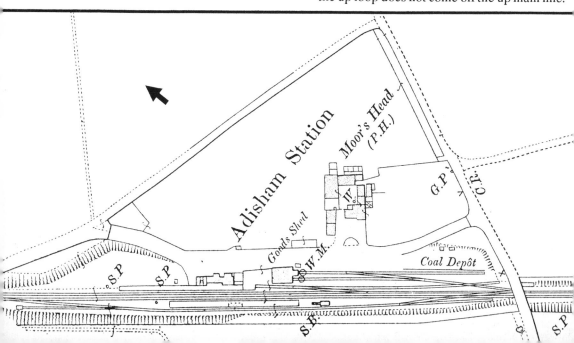

Adisham Station.

Published by
C.B. Hosking
Adisham.

42. The station was one of the busiest on the route and, although the village had only about 500 residents, the station served orchards, hop gardens and farms over a wide area, which included Wingham until the full opening of the East Kent Light Railway after WWI. (Lens of Sutton)

43. Three members of staff are evident as class 4 2-6-4T no. 42077 arrives with the 4.2pm from Dover on 13th September 1958. At this time there were three porters, three clerks, three signalmen and a station master. As with Bekesbourne, the station opened with the line and the main buildings were of similar design. (J.H.Aston)

44. Goods outward include three or four vans of fruit daily in season, raspberry canes, strawberry plants, sugar beet, barley and cattle. Arriving was coal, fertiliser, seed potatoes and agricultural machinery, an example of which is near class N1 no. 31878 as it passes on 2nd August 1958, incorrectly showing the Ramsgate headcode. The train is the 11.50am Victoria to Dover, an up goods train being less obvious beyond the footbridge which dates from about 1911. (J.H.Aston)

45. The goods yard closed on 7th May 1962 and the signal box followed on 25th February 1979, but the main building survived to be photographed in 1991. The goods shed was also still extant. In 1983, work started on converting the unstaffed premises to a training centre for the mentally handicapped. (J.Scrace)

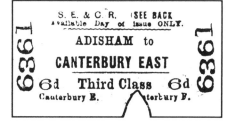

S. E. & C. R.   (SEE BACK
Available Day of Issue ONLY.

6361   ADISHAM to
CANTERBURY EAST
6361
6d   Third Class   6d
Canterbury E.   terbury E.

46. No. 47830 speeds through on 10th May 1991 with the 07.59 Liverpool to Folkestone Central, the station having one train call once each way each hour. No longer do seed boxes from John Harvey Ltd or watercress baskets adorn the platforms. In 1992 most of the station equipment was painted green by a local TV engineer who had leased the station for his business use and who provided a public waiting room at his own expense. (J.Scrace)

AYLESHAM

47. The halt was opened on 1st July 1928 to serve an extensive housing estate partially developed during the previous decade for miners at the nearby Snowdown Colliery. A shirt factory was established at Aylesham to employ their families, the output being despatched by rail from Adisham. (R.M.Casserley)

48. Electrification work and associated platform improvements were in progress when class L no. 31767 called with the 3.0pm from Faversham on 2nd August 1958. Traffic figures for 1936 showed that 54,000 people travelled between here and Dover. The Canterbury figure was 56,500, most passengers being of Durham, Welsh or Scottish origin, having moved from other pits. (J.H.Aston)

49. Prior to WWII, two private sidings for Aylesham Tennants Ltd. trailed off the up line, north of the platform. Seen in 1991, the new buildings date from 1968 and the footbridge from 1969. By 1992 staff was provided on weekday mornings only. (J.Scrace)

50. The halt was opened in 1914, although the sinking of two 18ft mine shafts had commenced in September 1906. The first coal was raised on 19th November 1912, from a depth of 1370ft. By 1917 the pit was over 3000ft deep, several seams in excess of 4ft. were being worked and over 3000 tons of good steam coal were being produced per week. A southward view in 1954 shows some of the colliery sidings on the left. (D.Cullum)

51. Platform replacement and extension was nearing completion when Q1 class no. 33039 stopped with the 12.3pm from Chatham on 13th September 1958. Behind its chimney is the National Coal Board locomotive shed and to the right are parts of the headgear, upturned mine cars and a concrete signal post. The suffix "and Nonnington" was used for many years. (J.H.Aston)

52. The colliery headgear is on the right and its standard gauge wagons are in the centre as N class 2-6-0 no. 31855 leaves with the 11.50am Victoria to Dover on 13th September 1958. The colliery had gone into receivership in 1923 before being acquired by Pearson & Dorman Long Ltd. During 1936 there were 137,000 passenger journeys between here and Dover, mainly miners commuting. (J.H.Aston)

53. Steam haulage was still employed by the NCB in 1977, ten years after it had ceased on BR. The loop (left) from the down line was wired for overhead electric supply to avoid the danger of the conductor rails in the yard. The 1927 Avonside locomotive is *St. Dunstan*, its companion being *St. Thomas*. (P.Horne)

Railfreight Construction
Snowdown Signal Box

54. The colliery closed on 23rd October 1987, and two years later coal mining in Kent ceased when Betteshanger ended production. The disused locomotive shed is visible as the 14.20 Victoria to Dover Western Docks approaches on 10th May 1991. The highlight of the day for platform staff used to be the arrival of students of the nearby physical education college. "Young Amazon Ladies" was the local description. (J.Scrace)

55. The fenced off down loop was still in place in 1992, by which date the box was staffed in peak hours only. The loop had been used for loading trains of the type seen in picture no. 65, the minestone having been transported during 1988-89 only. The colliery was producing 4-500,000 tons of coal annually in the 1950s and employing up to 2000 men. By the 1970s the average figures were 210,000 and 950, the output being halved in its final year. (J.Scrace)

SHEPHERDSWELL

56. The station opened with the line and served a community of about 400, this figure doubling in 1911 when colliery development was starting in the district. This northward view is from about 1903 and includes steps down to the foot crossing for passengers. (K.Elks coll.)

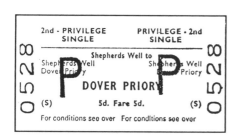

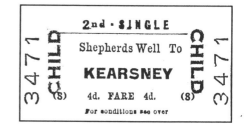

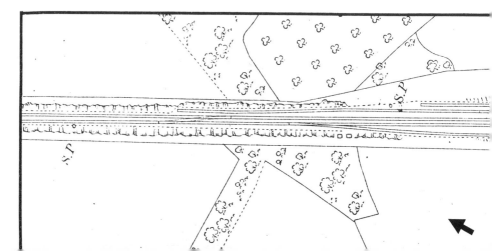

57. There has been inconsistency about the spelling of the name, the early railway companies and the Ordnance Survey using one word but the SR and BR using two. The earlier name of "Sibotswold" is often used by locals still. Ex-LSWR class T9 no. 314 passes under the bridge painters in about 1930. The structure had been erected in about 1911. (D.Cullum coll.)

The 1907 survey predates the East Kent Light Railway, the terminus of which was built in the field top centre. During WWII a gun siding was laid down in the vee of the junction and another placed north of the EKLR engine shed. The guns were stored in Lydden Tunnel when not in use.

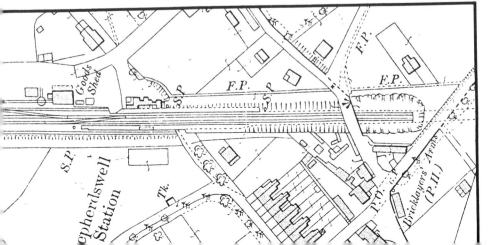

Other views and a later map of this station are included in a companion album, *East Kent Light Railway.*

58. The 12.6pm Faversham to Dover was headed by class L no. 31765 on 13th September 1958. It is passing the goods shed which con-tained a crane of 35 cwt capacity, as did all other sheds on the route. (J.H.Aston)

59. Arriving from the south on 23rd May 1959 is class O1 with a Railway Enthusiasts Club railtour of the former EKLR. It ran round its train on the main line and then hauled it along the track in the foreground. The nearest post would soon support an overhead conductor of the type seen in picture no. 53 but the up siding (in the background) had just been equipped with a conductor rail. (A.E.Bennett)

60. Photographed on the same day in the up platform was no. E5000, one of the new electric locomotives intended for use on boat trains and freight traffic. It is fitted with a panto-graph for use under overhead wires and collector shoes for use on conductor rails. (A.E.Bennett)

61. The 12.38pm freight from Dover to Faversham is ready to depart from the down platform on 8th July 1959. Type 2 diesel no. D5017 is in charge, this class being used only temporarily until the new type 3 locomotives arrived. Class O1 no. 31065 stands in the usual position for the branch engine. (J.H.Aston)

62. Electro-diesel no. E6017 rumbles over the crossover on 20th May 1967. The advent of these versatile locomotives rendered the overhead wiring obsolete and the fleet of 24 electric locomotives was fitted with diesel engines. General goods facilities were withdrawn on 10th June 1963 but coal traffic from Tilmanstone Colliery via the former EKLR route continued until April 1984, although the line was not officially closed until 1987. (J.N.Faulkner)

BRITISH RAILWAYS (S)
This ticket is issued subject to the Bye-laws,
Regulations and Conditions contained in the
Publications and Notices of and applicable to the
Railway Executive
Stonehall & Lydden Halt to ←
SHEPHERD'S WELL
Third Class. - Fare 3d.
NOT TRANSFERABLE. 2d

63. The east elevation retains details of its LCDR ancestry, notably the distinctive position of the glazing bars in the sash windows. The EKLR had an independent booking office on its own platform, from which the last passengers were carried on 1st November 1948. By 1992 BR provided a booking clerk on weekday mornings only. (C.Hall)

64. Ten motor luggage vans were built for the Kent coast electrification scheme, for use in boat trains. Batteries gave power on non-electrified dock lines. In the late 1980s, they were sometimes used singly for parcels or mail services, but by 1991 they were largely redundant, a few being retained for depot duties. The northern portal of Lydden Tunnel is in the distance, the entire bore being on a falling gradient of 1 in 132 towards Dover. (C.Hall)

STOCK LIST - JUNE 1992

STEAM

0-6-0ST	Fox Walker *Minnie*	1874
0-4-0ST	Barclay no. 2248	1948

DIESEL

0-4-0	Fowler		1952
0-6-0	English Electric		1967
0-4-0	Ruston & Hornsby	48DS	1951
0-4-0	" "	88	1952
0-4-0	" "	*Edwin*	1948
0-6-0	" "	RCT no. 427	1961
0-6-0	BR no. 08108		1953

COACHES

LMS brake/third	1936
Leyland prototype	1983
BR Mk I suburban no. E43140	

WAGONS

3 open wagons
6 box vans
2 tank wagons
2 flat wagons
2 brake vans
1 bogie van

65. Minestone from Snowdown passes south on 6th September 1988 behind nos. 33059 and 33204. The material was destined for Sevington, east of Ashford, from where it would be distributed by road to Channel Tunnel terminal construction sites. Above the brake van can be seen the connecting spur to the former EKLR route. (J.Scrace)

66. The East Kent Light Railway Association was formed in 1985 to save the remaining 2½ miles of track, and rolling stock began to arrive in 1990. Standing at the re-edged platform in 1991 is ex-BR diesel no. 08108, ex-RNAD van no. 161, ex-LMR brake van no. 49027, ex-NCB English Electric 0-6-0 and R&H 0-6-0 diesel no. 427. In 1992, a building was erected to the original design. (J.McKechnie)

67. Lydden Tunnel is 1 ml 609 yds long and was one of several tunnels in south-east Kent used for the storage of Naval munitions and the shelter of large rail-mounted guns during WWII, single line working being instituted for normal traffic. Class L no. 31766 emerges from the south end during the electrification work, the insulators having been positioned. Coal was first cut in Kent when a small seam was discovered during the construction of this tunnel, although commericial quantities were not found until 1884 when work first started on a Channel Tunnel. (P.Ransome-Wallis)

STONEHALL AND LYDDEN HALT

68. Shaft sinking at Stone Hall colliery started in 1913 but was curtailed by the advent of WWI. Subsequently the shafts were capped, no coal having been produced. The halt (centre right) was opened in 1914 and a siding (lower right) was laid, being mainly used to bring in bricks, millions being needed for shaft lining. (H.J.Patterson Rutherford coll.)

69. A northward view, shortly before closure of the halt on 5th April 1954, includes the points to the siding. The signal box remained in use until 3rd February 1957. (D.Cullum)

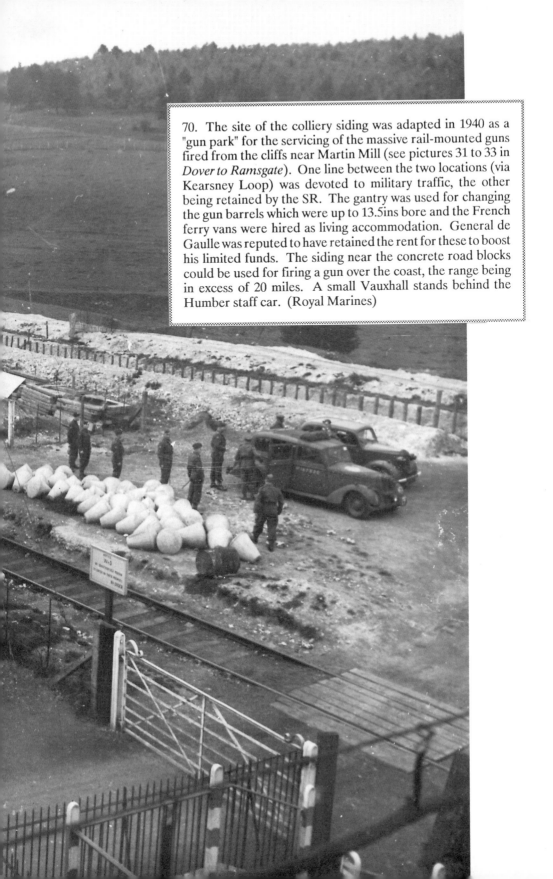

70. The site of the colliery siding was adapted in 1940 as a "gun park" for the servicing of the massive rail-mounted guns fired from the cliffs near Martin Mill (see pictures 31 to 33 in *Dover to Ramsgate*). One line between the two locations (via Kearsney Loop) was devoted to military traffic, the other being retained by the SR. The gantry was used for changing the gun barrels which were up to 13.5ins bore and the French ferry vans were hired as living accommodation. General de Gaulle was reputed to have retained the rent for these to boost his limited funds. The siding near the concrete road blocks could be used for firing a gun over the coast, the range being in excess of 20 miles. A small Vauxhall stands behind the Humber staff car. (Royal Marines)

KEARSNEY

71. The station was opened over a year after the line, on 1st August 1862 and was named Ewell until 1st February 1869. There were already two stations of this name in Surrey.

The 1872 edition shows two wagon turntables but fails to mark the track between them. No footbridge is marked as this was not erected

The LCDR ground signals are seldom seen closely. Note also that there are two down starting signals. (Lens of Sutton)

until 1886, having previously served at Chatham.

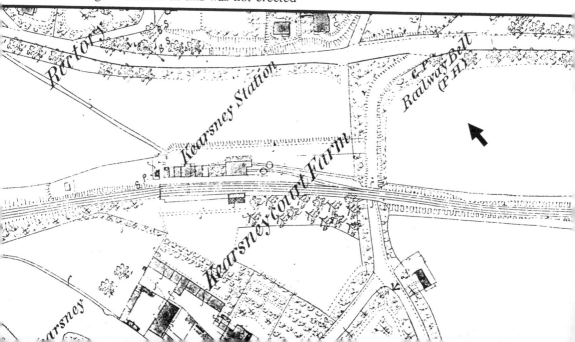

72. After 1882, the station became a fairly busy junction for Deal. Even after the opening of the joint line to Dover from that town, the SER still had the advantage of direct running between London and Deal until the LCDR introduced direct trains, diverging south of Kearsney. This northward view reveals that the up bay was signalled for starting passenger trains. (Lens of Sutton)

73. The absence of a tail light suggests that through coaches or a van are about to be attached to this up train. Specialists in sanitary architecture will note that the gentlemen's facilities are roofed with louvered ventilation all round. In 1895 this signal box was noted for having an unusual signalman. He was only 4ft tall. (Lens of Sutton)

74. When photographed on 8th February 1953 neither bay was signalled for passenger departures, but 4-4-0 class D1 no. 31247 is standing in the down one. It was waiting to pilot the next train for the Deal line, as the gradient in Guston Tunnel was 1 in 71. Piloting of diverted trains was necessary during the four month closure of the line through Herne Bay following flood damage. (D.Cullum)

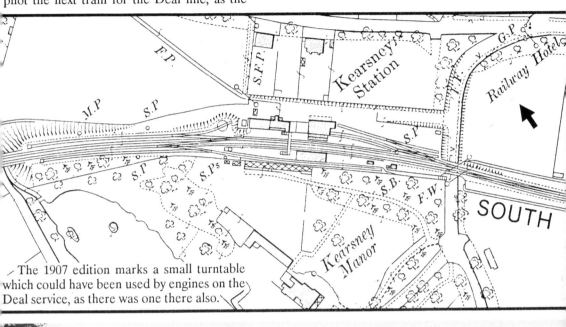

The 1907 edition marks a small turntable which could have been used by engines on the Deal service, as there was one there also.

75. The down sidings north of the station were reduced to one and this was sometimes used for the storage of empty coal wagons if the colliery lines were congested. This August 1956 photograph confirms that the station was gas lit, few rural locations having such luxury. (J.J.Smith)

76. The waiting shelter was still attached to the goods shed when pictured in September 1958 as conductor rails lie in the "four-foot". Freight service was withdrawn on 4th September 1961 but the signal box remained in use until 7th December 1980. (J.H.Aston)

77. Demolition of the shelter in 1979 revealed the old painted sign "Kearsney for River and Ewell" (right). Seen in 1989, the historic relic had been thoughtfully retained. Further platform improvements were then in progress. (V.Mitchell)

SOUTH OF KEARSNEY

78. Looking south at Deal Junction in 1953, we have the main line to Dover on the right with the Kearsney Loop to the Deal line on the left. This was authorised in July 1881 but was not opened until 1st July 1882. Regular use ceased in 1970 when the daily coal train from Shepherdswell to Richborough Power Station was withdrawn. The last passengers were in a Southern Electric Group railtour on 11th April 1971, closure being on 8th August following. The box closed on 11th February 1973. (D.Cullum)

79. Buckland Junction still exists, being the point at which the line from Deal joins our route in a trailing direction. The signal box remained in use until 7th December 1980, since which date the junction has been controlled from Dover Priory. (J.Scrace)

Just south of Buckland Junction were the Dover Gas Works sidings. Formed in 1821, the Dover Gas Company moved production to its rail-connected works in 1868. By 1914 they were taking 21,000 tons of coal per annum and, by 1937, 25,000 tons plus a large tonnage of gas oil by rail. South Eastern Gas Board took over in 1949 and modernised the works, including a much-improved rail layout. At its peak, before grid gas took over in the 1960s, Dover Works produced about 600 million cubic feet of gas per annum, for which the railway delivered some 40,000 tons of raw material. The railway had to compete with cheap sea freight, however, the SEGAS ships sometimes brought cargoes of gas coal directly to Dover. Gas production ceased in March 1971.

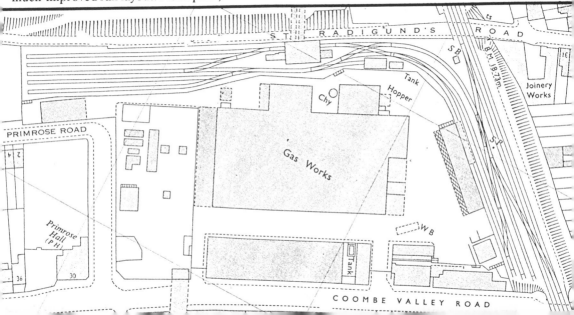

DOVER PRIORY

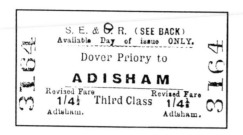

Other pictures and maps of this station are included in our *Dover to Ramsgate* album.

The longer part of the "Engine House" on this 1907 map was for carriage accommodation. The two platforms and running lines are spanned by a roof, the third track that passes under Folkestone Road being a goods loop.

The private siding to the Ordnance Depot was in use until about 1966. Opened on 22nd July 1861 as "Dover Town", the name was changed to "Dover Priory" in July 1863. The SER's station was already listed as "Dover Town".

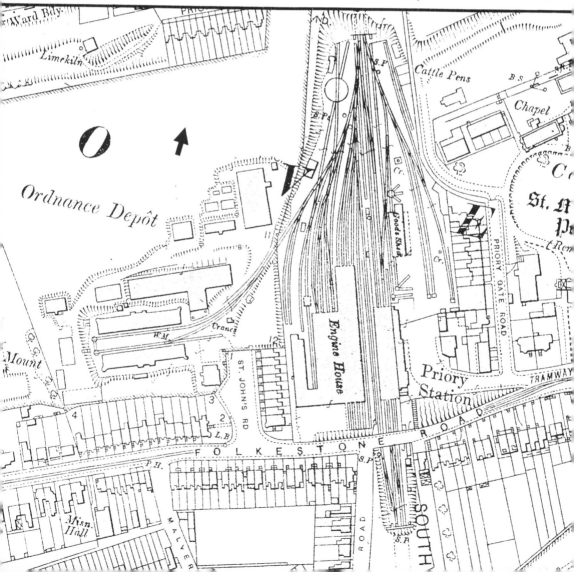

80. A 1932 photograph during the complete rebuilding of the station shows the new platform (no. 3), built to serve the former goods loop, this only being possible after the removal of the overall roof. The old offices and goods shed are evident on the right, the latter being succeeded by a new and larger shed to the left of this view. (H.J.Patterson Rutherford)

81. The old engine shed had four roads under two roof spans, the carriage shed being on the left. Seen on 14th May 1927 is class B1 no. A189, the A prefix having been applied by the SR to indicate that Ashford was responsible for maintenance. The shed was closed in 1928 when a new one opened on the coast. (H.C.Casserley)

82. The rebuilding included lengthy steel framed glazed canopies, an enclosed footbridge and luggage lifts, the tower of one being evident. Only the platform on the right remains to be surfaced. North of the station and in the distance is Priory Tunnel (158 yds). Charlton Tunnel, which is 264 yards in length, is further north. (British Rail)

83. Emerging from Priory Tunnel is class N15 no. 800 *Sir Meleaus de Lile*, the headcode indicating that it has run via Deal from Margate and is bound for London. The signal box was converted from mechanical operation and received a panel on 27th April 1980. The goods yard closed on 3rd July 1961 but some sidings were retained for berthing purposes and were still in use 30 years later. (D.Cullum coll.)

84. No. 47539 runs round a solitary van on 14th April 1990. Picture 64 has shown a MLV which took over this type of duty. That year they also began hauling pairs of oil tankers loaded with water from Dover Priory well to Ramsgate and Ashford depots where water shortage had caused closure of the carriage washers. (P.G.Barnes)

85. The 12.47 Dover Western Docks to Victoria is crossing to platform 1 on 14th April 1990, joining passengers thus being spared the climb over the footbridge. All three platforms are signalled for reversible running. Scissors crossovers are provided south of the station and two sets to the north. The station now handles passengers from the Eastern Docks brought in by bus, four non-stop trains to Victoria being added daily in 1987 for ferry, Seacat and hovercraft travellers. (P.G.Barnes)

DOVER HARBOUR

Top left on this 1866 map is the 684yd long Dover Harbour Tunnel from Dover Priory. This and the short line to the LCDR terminus (left of centre) opened on 1st November 1861, the single line extension onto Admiralty Pier (lower right) following on 21st December 1864. The rival SER already had such an extension from their terminus - Dover Town (lower centre). At this time there was no connection between the two companies here. Note the limited length of quayside siding. In 1869 two of the eight LCDR trains ran through to the pier, while in 1890 the figures were five and eleven respectively. By 1897 there were through coaches from Liverpool and Manchester. This and the next map have been reduced to 20" to 1 mile.

86. A terminus for its first three years only, the station was provided with a centre engine release road and a footbridge. Here we look towards Dover Priory. No.650 is an LCDR M class 4-4-0 and was in use from 1891 until 1926. (D.Cullum coll.)

87. Looking south in 1921 we see a line curving under the down platform, which was on wheels, as at Halesworth (see our *Branch Line to Southwold*, picture 33). The line ran to the Prince of Wales Pier and Eastern Docks. (Pamlin Prints)

88. A southward view from the up platform includes Hawkesbury Street (right), the signal box of that name, the 1881 level crossing over Elizabeth Street, and two footbridges, one in the left distance. Seen in September 1921, the gates on the left were redundant by then, the road crossing have been removed.
(Pamlin Prints)

89. The same site is viewed later from the south, as a train proceeds towards Dover Marine. The Elizabeth Street crossing has been closed but the gates have been mounted on wheels. On the left is the sign to the booking office. The station closed on 10th July 1927, the SER Town station having closed on 10th October 1914. (Lens of Sutton)

The 1907 edition has the 1902 Prince of Wales Pier running off the right margin. The line to it is shown passing under the down platform, running in Strond Street parallel to the Corporation's tramway track and passing over the swing bridge near Wellington Basin. Lower left is the double tracked curve which was opened on 15th June 1881 to allow SER trains access to the joint line to Deal.

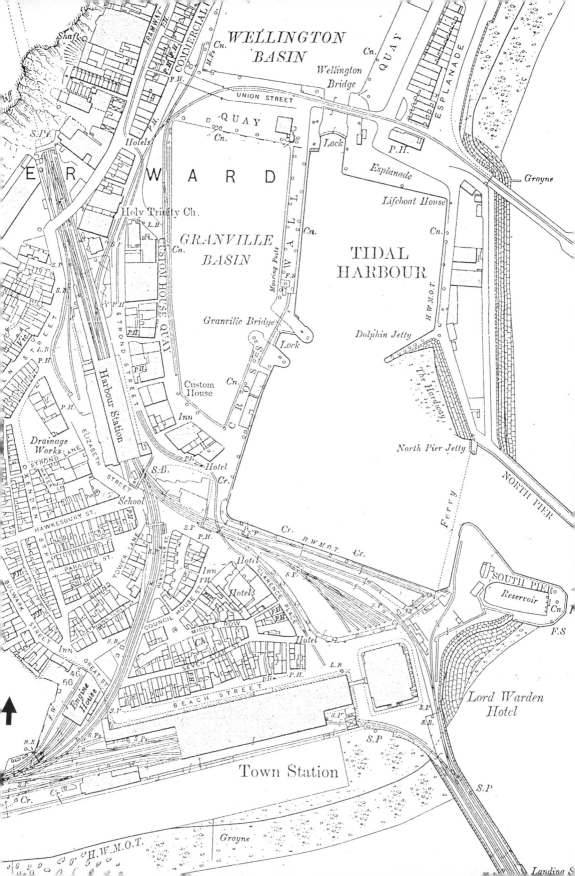

90. Photographed in June 1992, the western
part of the Harbour station was still standing,
along with the tower, the base of which is seen
in the previous picture. The building was in use
as a Sealink training centre. The bridge under
construction would carry the new A20 from
Folkestone, which then crossed the line at the
south end of Priory station. The signal box was
opened on 13th May 1934 and still retained its
lever frame in 1992. (V.Mitchell)

92. Boat trains from London ran onto the
Prince of Wales Pier in 1904-09 in connection
with transatlantic ships from Germany. The
platform canopy is obscured by the train and
the Q class 0-4-4T. The Admiralty subsequently had use of one side of the pier. Part
of the pier has now been incorporated into the
International Hoverport. (D.Cullum coll.)

DOVER HARBOUR BOARD

91. For most of their history the DHB was responsible for maintaining the lines in the foreground. Lower right is the 1902 line from Harbour station which passes over the Wellington Basin swing bridge and onto the Prince of Wales Pier. Lower left is the line to the Admiralty Dockyard and Eastern Docks. The adjacent tapered plot of land was occupied by houses (see map) until the bombing of WWII. In 1951, a direct connection from Wellington Bridge to the Eastern Docks was laid, avoiding reversals on the pier. Continental ferries and Dover Marine are at the top of the picture, while the train ferry berth is near the white buildings. Lower centre a siding curves to a former Ordnance Depot. (H.J.Patterson Rutherford coll.)

93. A 1958 view of class B4 no.30084 includes the old lifeboat station, which can be located in picture 91. The siding was used for wagons loading rubbish from the yachts moored in Wellington Dock. These ex-LSWR loco- motives were in regular use at Dover until 1957 and on standby until 1959, when they were found to be too close to the new conductor rail safety boards. (F.W.Ivey)

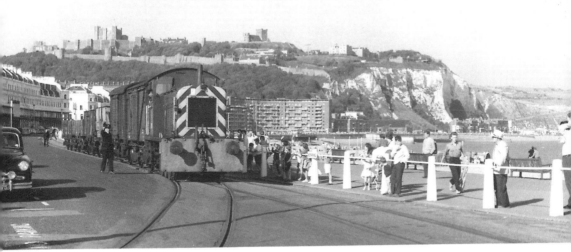

94. Class 04 diesels were used from 1957. This example is approaching the 1951 curve from The Esplanade to Wellington Bridge in July 1962. Two flagmen were required but they were powerless to take any action about cars parked on the track, by then a common problem. (A.A.F.Bell)

95. The route along The Esplanade and Waterloo Crescent was opened in July 1918, its main purpose being to serve the Admiralty Dockyard. Initially the track was above road level, but in 1924 the DHB relaid it as seen. (J.A.G.Coltas)

96. The Eastern Arm is visible as a class B4 proceeds west in 1958. After both world wars, the line carried large amounts of scrap steel from a ship breaking yard at the Eastern Docks. (F.W.Ivey)

97. Before the line turned onto the Eastern Arm there was a double track section. In this vicinity it served the Parker Pen factory (right) and an Esso oil depot. P class no. 31323 is now resident on the Bluebell Railway and named *Bluebell*. (F.W.Ivey)

98. In 1932, the SR established coal sidings on the former dockyard site and built a massive coal hopper with a wagon tippler for emptying wagons onto a conveyor. For a few years a big coal export business flourished, much to the annoyance of sea-front visitors and residents who had to suffer smoke from engines and coal dust blown from frequent 40-wagon trains running along the promenade. After WWII, oil traffic increased in its place but this diminished and the line closed on 31st December 1964. Pictures 23 and 24 in our *Dover to Ramsgate* album show the second hopper, which was supplied by aerial ropeway. (R.Hollingsbee)

Track diagram in 1957.

Marine Parade — Parker Pen Factory — Eastern Docks — Eastern Arm

99. The pier is on the right and is effectively the western arm of the harbour. At its landward end is the tall Lord Warden Hotel with the long roof of the SER Town station to the right of it. On the left is the frontage of the LCDR Harbour station, identifiable by its tall tower. The first part of Admiralty Pier was built in 1847-75, the part beyond the bend dating from 1897-1909. SER trains started to run onto it in 1859, LCDR services following in 1864. The detached part of the breakwater is still under construction and is connected to the Eastern Arm by a temporary bridge. (R.Hollingsbee coll.)

100. A train from the SER route shelters under the sea wall, the connection from their Town station being on the right. The 1864 single line from the LCDR Harbour station is on the left. Both lines had been connected in the 1870s. Train operation was controlled from Dover Pier box (left) by the Admiralty until 1892 and the DHB until 1914. (Lens of Sutton)

101. Prior to WWI, nearly 12 acres of land was made up by infilling the harbour on the east side of the Admiralty Pier. A boat train passes the new ground as it proceeds towards the end of the pier, which was used for ferries during the construction of the new station - to be known as Dover Marine. This is one of the SECR's E class 4-4-0s, first produced in 1906. (I.Gotheridge coll.)

DOVER MARINE

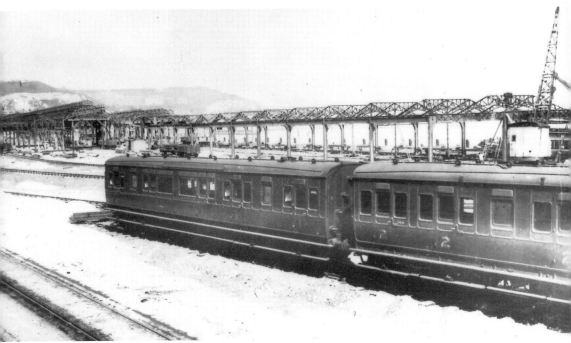

102. Viewed from the position of the people in the previous photograph, the construction was well advanced when recorded on 27th April 1914. The outbreak of WWI that year meant that work was speeded up so that the new facilities could be devoted to military traffic. Ambulance trains commenced on 2nd January 1915. Passenger services were maintained at Folkestone for the duration of the war. (Lens of Sutton)

103. After the war, the impressive stone arched entrance was completed - it still bears the initials SE&CR today. Public passenger services commenced on 18th January 1919 but few local trains used the station until 1970. Nos. 1 and 2 roads are between the station and the waterfront but they had no platforms or weather protection. (D.Cullum coll.)

104. The station at the outer end of the Admiralty Pier was little used when photographed in 1933. The tracks and numerous crossovers were still shown on the WWII control diagram. It was in this area that a new train ferry berth was opened in 1987. (H.J.Patterson Rutherford coll.)

105. A 1948 picture features class L no. 1778 returning from a trip to the end of the pier, the injector leak betraying its route. The straight sided coach was typical of the new boat train fleet introduced by the SR in the 1920s and unusual in having three classes. This example was produced by Maunsell for the SECR in 1921. (P.Ransome-Wallis)

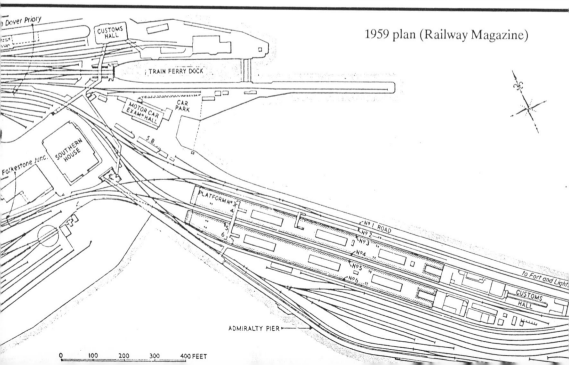

1959 plan (Railway Magazine)

to Dover Priory

CUSTOMS HALL

TRAIN FERRY DOCK

MOTOR CAR EXAM'N HALL

CAR PARK

S.B.

SOUTHERN HOUSE

Folkestone Junc.

PLATFORM N°3

N°1 ROAD

N°2

N°3

N°4

N°5

N°6

to Fort and Light

CUSTOMS HALL

ADMIRALTY PIER

0   100   200   300   400 FEET

106. Dover Marine box (right and in picture 103) was opened in 1914 and had 120 levers, only seven of which were spare. Class O1 no. 31434, seen on 19th May 1957, was totally obscuring the long covered footbridge which spanned the line from Dover Priory. It ran from the main entrance (left of the tender) to the customs hall and had to be resited prior to electrification. (A.E.Bennett)

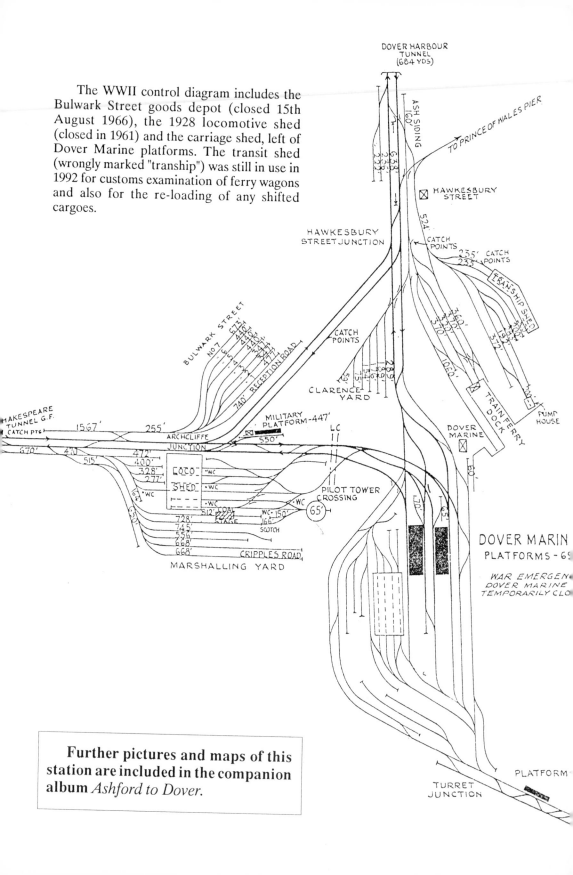

The WWII control diagram includes the Bulwark Street goods depot (closed 15th August 1966), the 1928 locomotive shed (closed in 1961) and the carriage shed, left of Dover Marine platforms. The transit shed (wrongly marked "tranship") was still in use in 1992 for customs examination of ferry wagons and also for the re-loading of any shifted cargoes.

Further pictures and maps of this station are included in the companion album *Ashford to Dover.*

DOVER HARBOUR
TUNNEL
(684 YDS)

ASH SIDING 160'

TO PRINCE OF WALES PIER

HAWKESBURY STREET

HAWKESBURY STREET JUNCTION

CATCH POINTS

255' CATCH POINTS

CATCH POINTS

TRANSHIP SHED

BULWARK STREET NO 7

RECEPTION ROAD

CATCH POINTS

CLARENCE YARD

TRAIN FERRY DOCK

DOVER MARINE

PUMP HOUSE

SHAKESPEARE TUNNEL G.F. CATCH PTS

1567'

255'

MILITARY PLATFORM - 447'

550'

ARCHCLIFFE JUNCTION

LC

670'

470'

515'

472'
400'
328'
277'

LOCO SHED

WC
WC
WC
WC

PILOT TOWER CROSSING

65'

COAL STAGE

728'
745'
556'
668'
668'

WC-150'
166'
SCOTCH

CRIPPLES ROAD

MARSHALLING YARD

DOVER MARIN

PLATFORMS - 69

WAR EMERGEN
DOVER MARINE
TEMPORARILY CLO

PLATFORM

TURRET JUNCTION

DOVER WESTERN DOCKS

107. "Marine" was changed to "Western Docks" on 14th May 1979. Seen in 1982, the unique train shed retained its special aura, although such signs as "Gentlemen Messieurs" had long gone, as had most of the track beyond the building. (F.Hornby)

108. As indicated in this 1990 photograph, the way out is via the footbridge. It does not divulge the length of the walk, the stone building in the distance housing the stairs down to the street. The platform extensions and canopies were added just prior to electrification in 1959. (A.C.Mott)

DOVER TRAIN FERRY

109. The train ferry berth (centre) was completed in 1936 after great engineering difficulties had been overcome. On the left is Dover Marine station and top centre is the 1851 Lord Warden Hotel, still extant but in use as offices since WWII. The building is a listed structure and may revert to hotel use. (P.Ransome Wallis coll.)

S. E. & C R   SEE BACK.
Available Day of Issue ONLY.

DOVER PRIORY to
DOVER HARBOUR

8075   1d   Third Class   1d   8075
Dover Har.   Dover Har

S. E. & C. R.   (SEE BACK
Ticket for One Perambulator, Child's Mail Cart, Small Invalid Chair, Sewing or Type-writing Machine.
Accompanied and at OWNER'S RISK.

DOVER HARBOUR to

1279   6 D.   any Station on the S.E.&C.R. not exceeding   1279
12 miles

S. E. & C R   SEE BACK
Available Day of Issue ONLY.

DOVER HARBOUR to

LONDON [S.E.&C.]

8776   6/5½   Third Class   6/5½   8776
London(S.E.&C.)   London(S.E.&C.)

→

111. The *Hampton Ferry* is seen leaving with freight vehicles, the main reason for the service. The companion vessels were the *Twickenham Ferry* and the *Shepperton Ferry*, all having been built by Swan Hunter, being 2839 tons gross. They each had a bow rudder and an aft bridge. (H.J.Patterson Rutherford coll.)

110. As there is a tide differential of about 25ft at Dover, a non-tidal berth was considered desirable. After warping the vessel in, the gate in the foreground was closed, and pumps (housed in the building on the right) adjusted the water level so that the link span was level. This operation could take up to 15 minutes. (S.W.Baker)

112. When built the gate was unusual in being totally submerged when open, the ship passing over it. The gate folded in the middle to lay flat on the floor of the dock. The boat contained a diver's helmet and a hand cranked air pump, all now long obsolete. (British Rail)

113. A view from a train ferry shows its four tracks converging into two on the link span and then diverging into five on the land. The now familiar LCDR tower is in the distance, as are various military buildings. (British Rail)

114. Looking from the bridge seen in the previous picture, we see the extent of the sidings in the early 1950s. On the left is the Dover Priory - Folkestone line, with the connection to Clarence Yard. On the right is the transit shed, which contained two sidings for customs purposes and load adjustments, as described. (P.Ransome Wallis)

115. Soon after the liberation of France the train ferry was back in service frantically shipping supplies to the advancing forces. The headboard reads "The 1000th British built War Dept main line locomotive shipped since D-Day". The photograph was taken on 9th May 1945, eleven months after the first landings. (British Rail)

116. Class C 0-6-0s were allowed inside the ferries. Surrounded by footbridges, no. 31243 performs her duties in 1958. Perishable foodstuffs from the Mediterranean area and mail made up much of the traffic. "Night Ferry" sleeping cars were conveyed from 14th October 1936 to 3rd September 1939 and from 15th December 1947 to 31st October 1980. (P.Ransome Wallis)

117. Having been hauled off the ship on 18th April 1954, the Paris to London sleeping cars are being propelled into Dover Marine, where they were attached to the 7.20am to Victoria. The shunter is holding a brake valve which is linked to the train brakes by a length of hose. The same device was used when shunting sleeping cars onto a ferry. Through cars from Brussels and Basle were also included in the train in some years. (N.Sprinks)

118. The carriage shed on the west side of the station was an obstacle to further development of the area. This 1987 photograph was taken just prior to its demolition, which would make way for a lorry park in connection with the new train ferry berth. Ferry vans were berthed here for a few months only. (E.Puddick)

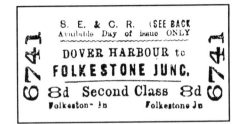

S. E. & C. R.   (SEE BACK
Available Day of issue ONLY
DOVER HARBOUR to
FOLKESTONE JUNC.
8d   Second Class   8d
Folkeston- Jn   Folkestone Jn

119. Four sidings were laid out west of the station and inside the bend of the Admiralty Pier to accommodate wagons joining or leaving the vessel. The promenade beyond the fence was seen earlier, in picture 104. No. 33203 is shunting on the afternoon of 14th April 1990, this locomotive having been subsequently preserved for use on the Swanage Railway. (P.G.Barnes)

120. The *Nord Pas de Calais* is operated by SNCF (French Railways). Traffic commenced in May 1988, the DHB investing over £10m in the terminal which includes long rail link spans. These, combined with locomotives more powerful than those of the 1930s, have obviated the need for a non-tidal berth. Annual traffic by train ferry exceeded one million tons in 1988 for the first time in the history of the service. The elongated twin parallel funnels of the 13700 tonne ferry are in the background. (Dover Harbour Board)

121. The final three pictures were taken on 8th June 1992, soon after the vessel had arrived from Dunkirk at noon. Two class 33s crept down the link spans to couple onto wagons in the centre roads, while lorries were unloaded above them. Coaches for the station and lorries for the ferry drive along the area occupied by cranes in picture 103. (V.Mitchell)

122. Having coupled up, the locomotives move forward in unison to ensure that the vessel is unloaded evenly. They return, attach to the next lines of wagons, pull forward and reverse down onto vehicles standing in the shorter outer sidings before making the final journey back to land. (V.Mitchell)

123. Vertical movement at the rail joints is achieved by steel bars set into the rails and loosely bolted. Some horizontal movement is accommodated by the tapered joints seen on the short span in the foreground, which is hooked to the ferry when berthed. The 167m long vessel can carry 1400t of road vehicles and 2400t of rail wagons and usually makes three return crossings daily, providing an important and speedy international link with mainland Europe. (V.Mitchell)

MP Middleton Press

Easebourne Lane, Midhurst. West Sussex. GU29 9AZ
Tel: (0730) 813169   Fax: (0730) 812601

Write or telephone for our latest booklist

BRANCH LINES

BRANCH LINES TO MIDHURST
BRANCH LINES AROUND MIDHURST
BRANCH LINES TO HORSHAM
BRANCH LINE TO SELSEY
BRANCH LINES TO EAST GRINSTEAD
BRANCH LINES TO ALTON
BRANCH LINE TO TENTERDEN
BRANCH LINES TO NEWPORT
BRANCH LINES TO TUNBRIDGE WELLS
BRANCH LINE TO SWANAGE
BRANCH LINE TO LYME REGIS
BRANCH LINE TO FAIRFORD
BRANCH LINE TO ALLHALLOWS
BRANCH LINES AROUND ASCOT
BRANCH LINES AROUND WEYMOUTH
BRANCH LINE TO HAWKHURST
BRANCH LINES AROUND EFFINGHAM JN
BRANCH LINE TO MINEHEAD
BRANCH LINE TO SHREWSBURY
BRANCH LINES AROUND HUNTINGDON
BRANCH LINES TO SEATON AND SIDMOUTH
BRANCH LINES AROUND WIMBORNE
BRANCH LINES TO EXMOUTH
BRANCH LINE TO LYNTON
BRANCH LINE TO SOUTHWOLD

SOUTH COAST RAILWAYS

CHICHESTER TO PORTSMOUTH
BRIGHTON TO EASTBOURNE
RYDE TO VENTNOR
EASTBOURNE TO HASTINGS
HASTINGS TO ASHFORD
SOUTHAMPTON TO BOURNEMOUTH
ASHFORD TO DOVER
BOURNEMOUTH TO WEYMOUTH
DOVER TO RAMSGATE

COUNTRY RAILWAY ROUTES

BOURNEMOUTH TO EVERCREECH JN
READING TO GUILDFORD
WOKING TO ALTON
BATH TO EVERCREECH JUNCTION
GUILDFORD TO REDHILL
EAST KENT LIGHT RAILWAY
FAREHAM TO SALISBURY
BURNHAM TO EVERCREECH JUNCTION
REDHILL TO ASHFORD
YEOVIL TO DORCHESTER
ANDOVER TO SOUTHAMPTON

SOUTHERN MAIN LINES

HAYWARDS HEATH TO SEAFORD
EPSOM TO HORSHAM
CRAWLEY TO LITTLEHAMPTON
THREE BRIDGES TO BRIGHTON
WATERLOO TO WOKING
VICTORIA TO EAST CROYDON
EAST CROYDON TO THREE BRIDGES
WOKING TO SOUTHAMPTON
WATERLOO TO WINDSOR
LONDON BRIDGE TO EAST CROYDON
BASINGSTOKE TO SALISBURY
SITTINGBOURNE TO RAMSGATE
YEOVIL TO EXETER
CHARING CROSS TO ORPINGTON
VICTORIA TO BROMLEY SOUTH
ORPINGTON TO TONBRIDGE
FAVERSHAM TO DOVER

LONDON SUBURBAN RAILWAYS

CHARING CROSS TO DARTFORD
HOLBORN VIADUCT TO LEWISHAM
KINGSTON & HOUNSLOW LOOPS
CRYSTAL PALACE AND CATFORD LOOP
LEWISHAM TO DARTFORD
MITCHAM JUNCTION LINES

STEAMING THROUGH

STEAMING THROUGH EAST HANTS
STEAMING THROUGH SURREY
STEAMING THROUGH WEST SUSSEX
STEAMING THROUGH THE ISLE OF WIGHT
STEAMING THROUGH WEST HANTS

OTHER RAILWAY BOOKS

GARRAWAY FATHER & SON
LONDON CHATHAM & DOVER RAILWAY
INDUSTRIAL RAILWAYS OF THE S. EAST
WEST SUSSEX RAILWAYS IN THE 1980s
SOUTH EASTERN RAILWAY

OTHER BOOKS

TILLINGBOURNE BUS STORY
MILITARY DEFENCE OF WEST SUSSEX
BATTLE OVER SUSSEX 1940
SURREY WATERWAYS
KENT AND EAST SUSSEX WATERWAYS
HAMPSHIRE WATERWAYS